Contents

Any words appearing in the text in bold, **like this**, are explained in the glossary.

Get writing poems!

Poems are a special, exciting type of writing. Poems can be written about anything. You can think of a poem as being like the words of a song – they are often quite short and packed with ideas. This book will help you write your own poems. All you need to do is add your imagination!

Features of a poem

A poem is not just a story chopped up into short lines. Here are some basic features that make up a poem:

- Poems should have **rhythm**. It is easiest to hear this rhythm when you read a poem out loud. It may have a clear, regular rhythm like a nursery rhyme, or it might have a less 'sing-song' pattern, which suits a more serious poem.

@ Activity – reading for rhythm

Find a book that contains poems by different poets. Collections like this are called anthologies. Try reading a selection of poems out loud. Can you hear rhythms in the lines as you read? Does this happen more in some poems than in others?

Think of the poems as songs. Try to read them so your voice picks up any 'up and down' sound of the words. This may sound silly, but it will help you hear the rhythm of the poem. Can you hear the rhythm in this **rhyming couplet**?

Yesterday, upon the stair
I met a man who wasn't there;
from 'The Little Man' by Hugh Mearns

It is not easy to **define** what a poem is. But if you read enough poems, you will soon learn what they are!

Get Writing!

Write that Poem

Shaun McCarthy

www.heinemann.co.uk/library
Visit our website to find out more information about **Heinemann Library** books.

To order:
☎ Phone 44 (0) 1865 888066
▤ Send a fax to 44 (0) 1865 314091
💻 Visit the Heinemann Bookshop at www.heinemann.co.uk/library to browse our catalogue and order online.

First published in Great Britain by Heinemann Library, Halley Court, Jordan Hill, Oxford OX2 8EJ, part of Harcourt Education.
Heinemann is a registered trademark of Harcourt Education Ltd.

Editorial: Lucy Thunder and Helen Cox
Design: David Poole and Susan Clarke
Illustrations: George Hollingworth
Production: Séverine Ribierre
Origination: Dot Gradations
Printed in China by W K T

ISBN 0 431 15212 8 (hardback)
07 06 05 04 03
10 9 8 7 6 5 4 3 2 1

ISBN 0 431 15219 5 (paperback)
08 07 06 05 04
10 9 8 7 6 5 4 3 2 1

British Library Cataloguing in Publication Data
McCarthy, Shaun
  Write that Poem. – (Get Writing)
  808.1
A full catalogue record for this book is available from the British Library.

Cover design by David Poole, with illustrations by George Hollingworth

The publishers would like to thank Rachel Vickers for her assistance in the preparation of this book.

Quotation on page 8 from Edwin Morgan, *Collected Poems* (1996), reproduced with permission of Carcanet Press Ltd. Quotations on page 12 from Seamus Heaney, *Death of a Naturalist* (1969) and page 26 from T. S. Eliot, *Collected Poems: 1909–1962* (1974), reproduced with permission of Faber and Faber Ltd.

- The language of poetry is packed with detail and meaning. Many poems are less than a page long. But, by choosing the right words, poets can say something interesting in a few lines.
- Poems find new and different ways of describing things. In a few words they paint a picture in the reader's mind.

What can poems be about?

Think about this list when you come to write poems of your own. It might give you some ideas of where to start.

- Poems are often descriptions of places, people, events and many other things.
- Poems can also tell stories.
- Poems are often written about something the poet actually did, saw or felt.
- Poems often express the poet's feelings – how something made them happy, sad, angry or peaceful.
- Poems sometimes contain 'confessions', where the poet admits to feelings he or she cannot talk about easily.

Collecting ideas

Poems can be about anything, but unlike other forms of writing, they can also be about nothing! Well, not really, but poems don't have to tell a story. They can describe a place, a mood or an idea. This actually makes choosing a subject for a poem quite difficult. So, where do you get your ideas from?

A writing journal

It is a good idea to keep a rough book where you can jot down ideas for poems as you have them. Look around you, listen to people, and write down the things you see and hear. Use all your senses of sight, hearing, touch, taste and smell.

Here are some things that might give you ideas:

- odd things you overhear
- films
- photos
- things you read
- things you dream about
- your memories
- strange objects
- your feelings
- stories you have been told
- places you visit.

You probably won't use all of the ideas you write in your journal when you come to write a poem, but that is fine. You can just choose the best ones.

Top tip

You could start by writing out your poem in rough. Leave plenty of space between the lines so you can make changes. Sometimes just playing about with ideas sets your mind racing and lines for a poem come into your head.

Word lists

It is fun to use unusual or unexpected words in your poems. A good place to start collecting words is to make word lists. Pick a **noun** you will use in your poem and list as many **adjectives** and **verbs** that you can that might go with it, like this:

CAT – sleek, tabby, jet-black, proud
– dozing, purring, stretching, scratching, stalking, spitting, weaving

See how the poet here has used interesting words to describe leaves fluttering in the wind:

The leaves had a wonderful frolic,
They danced to the wind's loud song,
from 'The Leaves in a Frolic', **Anon**

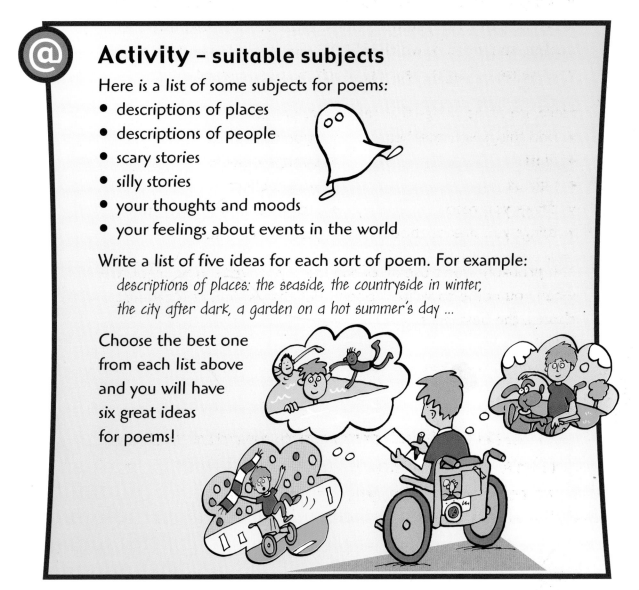

Activity – suitable subjects

Here is a list of some subjects for poems:
- descriptions of places
- descriptions of people
- scary stories
- silly stories
- your thoughts and moods
- your feelings about events in the world

Write a list of five ideas for each sort of poem. For example:

descriptions of places: the seaside, the countryside in winter,
the city after dark, a garden on a hot summer's day ...

Choose the best one from each list above and you will have six great ideas for poems!

Use your imagination

Did you know that poets sometimes tell lies?! They write about things that have never happened or they have never experienced. They actually use their imaginations to find new subjects for poems, and so can you.

Making things up

When you write a poem, you could pretend you were somewhere that you can not have been to. Here, the poet imagines they are an astronaut landing on another planet:

We come in peace from the third planet.
Would you take us to your leader?
Where we come from is blue and white
With brown, you see we call the brown
Here land, the blue is sea and the white is
Clouds over land and sea ...
from 'The First Men on Mercury' by Edwin Morgan

By using his imagination, this poet has shown us what people might say if they landed on a distant planet. He has made a situation that he has never experienced seem real through language. You could try writing a poem about a place or time that you can never go or have never been to – the Battle of Hastings, King Henry VIII's court or even the Moon!

Top tip

A way to let your imagination run wild is to look at all the people in the waiting room next time you are at the dentist. Who are they? Is that man reading a magazine a spy, waiting to have a special radio transmitter cemented into his teeth for a secret mission? Is that lady with the worn old coat actually a princess from Russia? You are imagining who people can be by looking at the real people you can see.

Using real events

As a poet, you can take things that really do happen to you and develop them. You can use your imagination to make them into interesting ideas for poems. For example, you could think about a football game you have played, and write a poem about it as if it was the World Cup.

@ Activity – creative thinking

Imagine you are going into a city on a double-decker bus. You are upstairs and the whole city appears in front of you.

This event is your starting point. Now use your imagination. What could make this view ahead of you more exciting? Maybe:

- you are going to meet someone for the first time, or see someone you have not seen for years
- you are starting a new school there
- it is somewhere you have never been before – maybe your family came from this place and you are making your first ever trip back.

Use one of the ideas and write the first four or five lines of the poem. If you think your ideas are really interesting, go on to write the rest of the poem.

Playing with words

Most poems are quite short so you need to make every word count. Think carefully about the **vocabulary** you use. When you write a poem look at each word and think: Do I know a more interesting word that could replace it?

Interesting words

Try to use interesting **adjectives** in your poems. If you are writing about the seaside you could say, *the sea was blue*. But instead you could picture the sea in your mind and describe it as green, *like the glass of an old green bottle*. This is much more imaginative and interesting.

Nonsense sentences

Don't be afraid to be inventive when you write your poem. Try putting together words that don't usually go together to surprise your reader, like *his shoes are like pink bananas*.

You could also try making up some nonsense sentences. They can be funny, but should have a purpose. You might write a poem in which different animals talk. The way they talk can echo the real sounds animals make. Monkeys can speak in a sort of nonsense chatter:
I'm a baboon and I bibble and babble.

Lions might speak in slow groans and growls:
We lions like to lie and loaf after lunch,
Where we munch on a haunch of whatever we hunt.

Top tip

Try to use strong, expressive words in your poems. These make more impact on the reader. For example, instead of saying 'walks along' you could say 'rushes along'. Or instead of 'cuts the air' you might say 'slices the air'.

Using a thesaurus

One way of finding alternative words for poems is to look up the word you want to replace in a thesaurus. This is a book that groups together words that mean roughly the same thing. For example, if you look up the word 'attack' you will find words like assault, raid and onslaught listed with it.

@ Activity – word games

Make a list of twenty words you would connect with cooking and food.

Use at least ten of these in a short poem about a visit to the seaside in summer. (Obviously the sun will be 'boiling hot'!)

Now do it the other way round. Make a list of at least twenty words you would use in a poem describing the beach in summer. Use these to write a poem about a busy restaurant kitchen, full of heat and hurry. The ideas below might help you.

A speedboat 'carves' through the sea. The wake curls back 'like icing round a cake'.

Cauldrons bubble like a 'sea full of swimmers'. It is 'hotter than any beach at midday'.

Making comparisons

You can create new and interesting **images** in your poems by comparing one thing to another. The connections are often unexpected, and make the reader see things in a new way.

Similes

A **simile** is a way of comparing two things using the words 'as' and 'like'. You will find these two little words in lots of poems. For example:

> the horse could run <u>like</u> the wind
> the road was straight <u>as</u> an arrow

See how 'as' and 'like' are used to join the two parts of the simile together.

Some similes have become part of our language, for example: *dry as a bone*. One of the main jobs of a poet is to invent new, exciting images. Describing an ancient battle, one poet wrote of arrows falling '*like showers of lazy summer bees …*'. This simile suggests lots of arrows travelling like a swarm of bees.

Metaphors

A **metaphor** is where one thing is described as if it actually were something else. This creates a vivid image. A metaphor can be very simple, for example: *a glaring mistake*. Metaphors can be more complex too. A poet once described an injured person as '*wearing a poppy bruise*'. He was linking the colour and shape of the bruise to the red bloom of a poppy.

Similes

Imagine a summer's day in a school where:
> The teacher drones like a buzzing fly,
> Pupils slump like dozing cats,
> The room is hot as a furnace.

Metaphors

Imagine a summer's day in the park where:
> The clouds are floating cushions,
> Boats glide on the lake's mirror,
> Ice creams are melting volcanoes.

Top tip

You can change a simile to a metaphor by taking out the 'as' or 'like'. For example, instead of saying 'the ship sailed through the waves like a plough' you could write, 'the ship ploughed through the waves'. Here, the ship has become a plough.

Activity – inventing images

Imagine a full, smelly dustbin in a back alley.

Make a list of five similes and five metaphors to describe it. Use all your senses of sight, smell, hearing, touch – perhaps even taste!

Now make some similes or metaphors for the following subjects:
- a lion stalking through the jungle
- a haunted castle in the moonlight
- a school hall full of noisy students
- a busy city street on Saturday morning.

The windows are closed like blind eyes. The moon is pale as a ghostly lantern. Shadows lie in corners like black snow. The castle seems tall as a cliff.

Write me a picture

When you write a poem, you use words to create a picture of something. This could be how a place looks, or the excitement of an event. Bring together all the things we have talked about so far to paint a picture with words:

- Use your imagination to 'see' the scene in your mind and make it come alive.
- Experiment or play with words and use them in unusual ways.
- Create **images** by using **metaphors** and **similes**.

Top tip

When you are describing something, don't just use your sense of sight. What can you hear, smell, even touch or feel? If you are describing a holiday beach, bring in the sound of the waves and people shouting; the smell of fish and chips; the feel of hot sand and the sun on your skin.

Personification

Personification is when you write about an object as if it has human qualities – for example: *the moon looks down on us*. This makes the moon sound as if it is a person up in the sky. Personification lets you describe objects in unusual ways. It is a good way to make a vivid picture in your reader's mind.

Word sounds

You can use the sounds of words to help you paint your word picture. Using words that start with the same letter or sound is called **alliteration**. For example: *the silvery moon shone on the sea*. The soft 's' sound creates an atmosphere of stillness and echoes the sound of the sea.

Alliteration

Apples are rosy and red, rich and ripe.
Slow and silent, the snake slithered.

Some words sound like their meaning, such as 'crunch' or 'splash'. This is called **onomatopoeia** and it can make your descriptions come alive – for example: *Hissing waves made shingle rattle and clatter.*

Activity – painting with words

Imagine you are on board an old-fashioned sailing ship in a storm.

Brainstorm a list of words that you might use to describe the scene. You could look at a book about ships and copy out some words, such as the names of the sails and masts.

Now write an eight-line poem describing the storm. Think about what you would see and the sounds you hear. How does the storm make you feel – excited or afraid, or both?

Imagine these things:
seeing – the rolling ship, the heaving sea, a loose rope blowing
*   to and fro ...*
hearing – the waves, the flapping sails, the shouts of sailors
*   and the creak of timbers ...*

Want to rhyme?

Many well-known poems rhyme. The word at the end of one line rhymes with the word at the end of one or more lines. Using rhyming words will help you create a sort of music in the words.

A simple pattern

A simple pattern for rhymes is a four-line **verse**. The words at the end of lines one and two rhyme. A second rhyme is made at the end of lines three and four, like this:

> *Way down south where bananas grow,*
> *A grasshopper stepped on an elephant's toe,*
> *The elephant said, with tears in his eyes,*
> *'Pick on someone your own size.'*
> from 'The Elephant', **Anon**

Finding the rhymes

The pattern of rhyming words is called the **rhyme scheme**. There is a simple way of marking the rhymes in a poem. Use the letters of the alphabet and work from the start of the poem. Put an A at the end of the first line, and an A beside the line or lines that rhyme with it. Then put a B at the end of the next different rhyme, and another B beside the lines that rhyme with that, and so on.

Here is part of a poem with the rhyme scheme marked up:

How does it know,	A
this little seed,	B
if it is to grow	A
to a flower or a weed,	B
if it is to be	C
a vine or shoot,	D
or grow into a tree	C
with a long deep root?	D

from 'The Seed' by Aileen Fisher

Top tip

Look in your school library for a rhyming dictionary. It groups together words that rhyme with each other. Most poets have one close by them when they are writing rhyming poems.

Clever rhyming

You don't have to use single **syllable** words ('cat' and 'bat') for all your rhymes. Two syllable words ('display' and 'today') and even three syllable words ('exploring' and 'ignoring') work well.

Activity – rhyming away

Imagine arriving at a theme park with some friends.

Write a short four-line poem describing your day out. Use a simple rhyme scheme, ABAB – lines one and three rhyme; lines two and four rhyme.

The roller coaster climbs into the sky.
People on the ground look up and wave.
It feels as if we might begin to fly –
Suddenly, I don't feel so brave!

Find the beats

Poems can have a very 'sing-song' **rhythm**. Within each line, the words are often arranged to create a strong rhythm or beat. Rhythm is an important part of all poems. You need to think about the rhythm of words as you write your poems. It makes poems different to **prose** writing.

Syllables

The individual sounds within a word are called **syllables**. For example, 'boy' or 'girl' each have one syllable, 'darkness' has two syllables, and 'confusing' has three syllables. If you say these words aloud slowly, you will hear each syllable.

Using the stresses

When we speak, we **stress** one or more syllables in a word. That means we say one part more strongly than the rest. When we say 'happy' we stress the first syllable 'ha–ppy.' When we say 'delight' we stress the second syllable, 'de–light. In poetry, these stresses are used to give poems rhythm.

Read this poem aloud and clap out the beats:

If you should meet a crocodile,
Don't take a stick and poke him;
Ignore the welcome in his smile,
Be careful not to stroke him.
from 'If you should meet a crocodile…', **Anon**

👍 **Top tip**

If a line in your poem has more than six stressed syllables, it should probably be two lines. See if you can break it into two shorter ones.

Can you hear the rhythm? What you were reading was stressed like this:

> If <u>you</u> should <u>meet</u> a <u>croc</u>-o-<u>dile</u>,
> Don't <u>take</u> a <u>stick</u> and <u>poke</u> him;
> Ig-<u>nore</u> the <u>wel</u>-come <u>in</u> his <u>smile</u>,
> Be <u>care</u>-ful <u>not</u> to <u>stroke</u> him.

See how the words or syllables are stressed according to how they are used in a line. If you stress any other words or miss any of these stresses out, it sounds odd. Now try reading the poem with the stresses on the words that are not underlined. How does it sound?

@ Activity – have you got rhythm?

Write a four line poem, with rhymes, giving an excuse for not doing your English homework.

Check that your lines have the same number of syllables, and the same number of stressed ones. You could make a pattern the same as the crocodile poem.

Now read your poem aloud. You should be able to hear the rhythm.

I'm sorry sir, I haven't done the test.
I mean, I did, but then our neighbour's dog
Dashed in and ate my book, he's such a pest.

Limericks

Some poems, especially funny ones, sound best when **rhythm** and rhyme work together. Limericks are a good example of how these two elements work together.

What are limericks?

Limericks are five-line poems written with a **rhyming scheme** and a bouncing sort of rhythm. Limericks look simple, but they must follow a strict pattern if they are to work.

Limericks are always funny and often rather rude. Here is an example of one that isn't rude!

There once was a man of Bengal
Who was asked to a fancy dress ball;
He murmured: 'I'll risk it
and go as a biscuit …'
But a dog ate him up in the hall.
                'Bengal', **Anon**

Patterns

Let's use what we have learnt about rhyme and rhythm to work out how this poem was put together.

- Lines 1, 2 and 5 rhyme, as do lines 3 and 4. So, the **rhyme scheme** is AABBA.
- Lines 1, 2 and 5 all have three stressed **syllables** – (*There once was a man of Ben-gal*).
- Lines 3 and 4 both have six syllables and two stresses (*and go as a bis-cuit*).

Top tip

Think carefully about punctuation at the end of lines – the end of a line is a sort of pause. A comma makes a longer pause, and a full stop an even longer one.

Clever rhymes

Really clever poets can use a mix of long words and short words to make a complex rhyme. Say 'stay at home', 'eat a bone' and 'telephone' out loud. You will find that as well as rhyming on the last words or syllable ('home', 'bone', 'phone') these little phrases and the long word are all made up of three syllables with similar sounds.

Using words with the same **vowel** sounds together can make a sort of half-rhyme sound, called **assonance**. See how the vowel sounds create a rhyme here: *She sees the falling leaves.*

@ ## Activity – *A man at a beach in Torquay*

Try writing a limerick about what you see happening in this picture – use your imagination too! Then read your limerick out loud to test it. Here are some words to help you, and the title of the activity could be your first line.

- line one ends with Torquay
- line two ends with sea
- line three ends with gusty
- line four ends with dusty
- line five ends with flee.

Writing in verses

When you write a story, you use a new paragraph each time the story moves to a new idea, time or scene. You start a new paragraph each time the story moves forward into a new topic. In some poems, **verses** do the same job as paragraphs. Verses are also called **stanzas**.

Verses can help you break up a poem. They make a longer poem easier for the reader to follow. Ballads are poems that tell stories. Ballads are broken up into verses to separate what is happening in the story. These two-line verses are about a fairy tale villain who rushes over rooftops at night:

> *Spring-heeled Jack, with cheeks like razors,*
> *A top-hat sleek as the tiles where he glides,*
>
> *Swoops to the kerb on a moonlit spot,*
> *Tips his brim and smiles like stars,*
>
> from 'Spring-Heeled Jack', by Shaun McCarthy

Making verses

One way of starting to organize your poem is to make a plan. Make a note of what you want to write about in each verse. You don't have to follow your plan exactly – you can always change it as you write. If you think of something extra to write about, your plan will help you decide where to put it.

Some poems have a different number of lines in each verse. It is a good test of your skills to try to write a poem where every verse has the same number of lines.

> *Plan for 'A day at the seaside'*
>
> *Verse 1 – sights, sounds and feelings on the journey*
>
> *Verse 2 – description of the beach*
>
> *Verse 3 – account of climbing the rocks, how I felt and what I saw*
>
> *Verse 4 – feelings about going home and thoughts about the day*

Activity – a story in verses

Look at the strip cartoon below. It tells a simple story in
four parts.

Write a four-verse poem using the cartoon as a guide. Each of
your verses must have the same number of lines, not less than
four, not more than eight. Imagine the story is happening to you.

Here is a first verse:

> We told our friends it wouldn't take all day,
> But when we started everything seemed bigger.
> The mountain towered right up to the sky,
> But we set off, said we'd be back by dinner!

When we started everything
seemed bigger ...

... and steeper ...

... and wetter ...

... but we reached the top!

Hearing voices

When we write a poem we usually write as ourselves. But you can write a poem as though you are someone else. For example, you might imagine you are an old wizard and take on the voice of that person or character.

Direct speech

When you write speech in a poem, use **direct speech**. This makes it more exciting. Direct speech means you write down exactly what you imagine your character saying. This gives the effect of things actually happening as we read. For instance:

> It's getting dark,
> the wind is blowing harder.

sounds more exciting than

> He said it was getting dark
> And the wind was blowing harder.

Different voices

You can also write a poem with two voices. Here different lines or **verses** are spoken by two different people. You might need different voices in:

- a poem where two people meet and talk, like two friends
- a poem in which different people give different replies to a question, such as a teacher asking pupils in the class what they would do if they won the Lottery
- a question and answer poem, such as a fairytale where a hero has to answer questions on his travels.

Top tip

If you are writing as someone else, think about how they would speak. A mad scientist would use complicated words. An elderly person might use old-fashioned words. An excited person would use short snappy words like 'It's great!' or 'Let's go!'

@ Activity – too much jelly

Look at the four characters mentioned below. They are at a school assembly. Using the notes below to help you, write a poem in different voices.

- The headteacher wants to know who filled the science teacher's car with jelly by pouring it through the sunroof. What he says in the assembly will be the first two lines of a poem.

- Ms James, the deputy head, is trying not to laugh. Write two more lines about what she says to the school.

- Tom was the one who filled up the car with jelly. In two more lines explain what he is thinking and why he did it.

- Anisha saw Tom do it. In the last two lines of the poem write what she feels about it.

You will end up with eight lines of poetry. Try to make each person sound different so that someone reading the poem will know what sort of characters they are. Also, remember to write what the characters say to each other in direct speech.

Free verse

Many poems do not rhyme and they have lines of different lengths. This is called **free verse**. Free verse poems do have a **rhythm**, but not a fixed regular one. Here is an example:

> *The winter evening settles down*
> *With smell of steaks in passageways.*
> *Six o'clock.*
> from 'Preludes' by T. S. Eliot

How does free verse work?

In free verse, you can change the **line lengths** and rhythm to suit the changing mood of the poem. A poem might start with short, sharp lines to describe something quick and busy (pupils hurrying into school at the bell). Then it might go on to have longer lines for describing something slow (a boring lesson on a hot afternoon).

Describing with sounds

Use the sounds of the words to help you describe things in free verse. Try to make the pattern of words echo what you are describing. For example, if you are writing about slow moving traffic you could say: *Cars crawl, red lights flash, stop, go, stop.*

This line has lots of short words and **stressed syllables**. The hard sounds of words like 'flash', 'stop' and 'go' show how the cars are stopping and starting.

Top tip

Think about the following things when you write free verse:
- do not let lines become too long
- think carefully where each line should end
- always read your free verse out loud to make sure it still sounds like poetry.

If you want to write about something still and silent, use soft words. See how this poet has created a calm and quiet poem by using words like 'feathery', 'soft' and 'whispers':

> Feathery soft and quiet the snow;
> It covers the road
>   and the walk
>   and the rooftops
>   and whispers to the world:
>   Shhh!

from 'Snow' by Margaret R Moore

Free verse sounds easier to write because it does not rhyme or have a regular rhythm. It is actually very difficult. Free verse still needs to have an interesting rhythm. The best way to get a feel for how to write free verse is to read lots of it.

@ Activity – write freely

Imagine a busy city street full of cars and shoppers, brightly lit store windows and street performers. Maybe it is Christmas Eve.

Write eight lines of free verse describing the scene. Pack the lines with ideas. Describe the sights, sounds and atmosphere.

Polishing your poem

When you have finished writing a poem, read it aloud to hear what it sounds like. Most poets make many changes so that their poetry is more polished. You can use the checklists below to help you decide if your poem is as good as it can be:

- Does every line say something interesting?
- Could any word be replaced with a more unusual one?
- Try to imagine you are reading the poem for the first time. Do you need to explain anything so that readers understand what you are writing about?
- What feelings are you trying to get across to a reader – laughter, sadness? Can you do anything to increase this feeling?

Top tip

Look for lines where you described something simply, but in a boring way. Try replacing these with a **simile** or **metaphor**. If you said that 'the insects hummed', would 'insects buzzed like distant traffic' work better?

How does it sound?

- Does your poem have a good **rhythm**?
- Do some lines sound too short? You probably need to add a word or even an **image**.
- Do some lines seem to go on too long? You might need to cut something out.
- Are there lines where you just keep stumbling over some words? If so, don't worry about changing them.

Poetry reading

Presenting your poem

Poems look good and are easier to read when they are laid out clearly.

- Use a wide margin on the left-hand side of you page. Start your lines further in than you would start a story. Be careful not to make the left margin so wide that your lines run over onto a second line!
- Leave a gap between each **verse** of your poem.
- If you are writing your poem, make sure your handwriting is neat and clear.
- Make sure your spelling, grammar and punctuation are correct. If you are using a word processor, try using the electronic spellchecker.

@ Activity – shapely poems

It can be fun to write poems in special shapes.

Try writing a poem about an aeroplane and lay it out to look like it is flying. You could use lots of very short lines to make its body, then a few longer lines for the wings. Here is a **shape poem** as an example.

The plane flies fast as lightning – it really is quite frightening
with sleek steel wings
and wheels, and guns like stings

Glossary

adjective word that describes a noun, for example <u>grey</u> *clouds*

alliteration putting together words starting with the same letter or sound. For example, *a slithery snake slid.*

Anon word used where the author of a poem is unknown

assonance putting together words with the same vowel sounds, for example *how now brown cow*

brainstorm to come up with lots of different ideas or words about a subject

define explain the meaning of a word. Dictionaries define words.

direct speech writing down the exact words a person says. In prose this is shown by speech marks, like this: *'This soup is hot!'*

free verse poetry that does not use traditional forms of rhyme and rhythm

image descriptive 'word picture' in which language is used in an imaginative way

line length number of words or syllables that create a line

metaphor description of something as if it were something else. Metaphors are used in poetry to make images.

noun a word used to name someone or something, for example *Lucy* and *letter* are nouns.

onomatopoeia words that sound like their meaning, for example, *plop* and *ping*

prose ordinary writing – anything that is not poetry or the script of a play

rhyme scheme pattern of rhymes at the ends of the lines of a poem

rhyming couplet two lines of poetry of the same length that rhyme together

rhythm like the beat in music. The rhythm in poetry is created by stressed and unstressed syllables.

shape poem poem where the layout of the words reflects what the poem is about. For example, a poem about a tree might be laid out to look like a tree.

simile comparing two things to make an image, using 'as' and 'like'. For example, *the sun was like a furnace.*

stanza another word for a verse of a poem

stress a stressed word or syllable in a word is one that we naturally say more loudly when we speak. In the word *annoy* we stress the second syllable, *ann—oy.*

syllable the individual sounds that make up words. For example, the word *mat* is one syllable, *terrifying* is four.

verb word that describes an action that someone in a sentence does, for example he *runs*, she *was walking*

verse a section of a poem separated from the verse before and the one after it by leaving a line

vocabulary the range of words used in a poem

vowel there are five vowels – a, e, i, o, u

Find out more

Here are some books with more poems to enjoy.

The Works, Paul Cookson (Macmillan Children's Books, 2000). Contains all kinds of poems from fables to free verse.

The Oxford Book of Story Poems, Michael Harrison and Christopher Stuart-Clark (OUP, 1999). Each poem in this book tells a story.

Revolting Rhymes, Roald Dahl (Puffin Books, 2001). Poems from one of Britain's favourite authors.

Websites

http://www.poetryzone.ndirect.co.uk/index2.htm
A website containing poems by children, information on more sites and ideas and resources.

Index